PASTA
COOKING

Photography by Peter Barry
Recipes by Judith Ferguson, Patricia Payne and Fréderic Lebain
Designed by Richard Hawke
Edited by Jillian Stewart

3260
© 1993 Coombe Books
This edition published in 1994 by Coombe Books for
Parragon Book Service Ltd
Unit 13-17, Avonbridge Trading Estate
Atlantic Road, Avonmouth, Bristol BS11 9QD
Printed and bound in Hong Kong
ISBN 1-85813-145-6

PASTA
COOKING

PARRAGON

Contents

Introduction

The rise in the popularity of pasta has been immense over the last few years. A greater interest in foods of other nations is the result of the increased migration of people and ideas, so it is hardly surprising pasta has become so fashionable.

Pasta is literally a paste made with flour and eggs. Commercial pasta is mainly made from a hard wheat called durum wheat, but fresh pasta may be made with any kind of flour. It can also be made in a variety of different colours with the addition of ingredients such as spinach and tomato purée.

Pasta is still freshly made in many Italian homes and many people have taken it up here, too, but you may find it more convenient to buy the fresh varieties now widely available in supermarkets. In addition to this a wide range of dried, packaged pastas are also on offer, but these do not match the taste of the real thing! Pasta comes in a bewildering array of shapes, and their Italian names often vary depending on which region they originate. For this reason it is often easier to look for the shape of the particular pasta you require, rather than the name.

Pasta is perfectly designed to be mixed with other ingredients. It can simply be mixed with olive oil and garlic or fresh herbs, or it can be enhanced with everything from tomatoes and cheese to ham and olives. Tomatoes are the most common ingredient, along with cheese and herbs, but even within these categories there are numerous flavours and uses. Parmesan is treasured for its wonderful flavour, while ricotta is perfect for stuffing pasta as it adds body and holds its shape well. One of the joys of cooking pasta is that it combines so well with numerous ingredients, so experiment with your favourites to find flavours which you enjoy.

One of the bonuses of pasta is that it is simple and quick to cook and there are only a few points to bear in mind. Never overcook pasta as it will quickly turn into a congealed mess. It is also prudent to remember here that fresh pasta cooks more quickly than the dried variety. Wholemeal pasta also takes longer to cook and the cooking time will also vary according to the thickness of the pasta. If the pasta is to be boiled, it should be in a large, uncovered saucepan of boiling, salted water with a little olive oil added to prevent the pasta sticking and the water boiling over.

The ease of cooking and variety of shapes and flavours offered by pasta ensures that pasta is here to stay, so start experimenting with some of the recipes in this book, and you will find producing the perfect pasta dish is simplicity itself.

MEATBALL SOUP

*A hearty soup which is almost a
meal in itself served with bread.*

SERVES 4

450g/1lb beef bones
1 carrot, peeled
1 onion, chopped
1 stick celery, chopped
1 egg, beaten
225g/8oz minced beef
60g/2oz breadcrumbs
Salt and pepper
1 tbsp oil
400g/14oz tin plum tomatoes
180g/6oz soup pasta
1 tbsp chopped parsley

1. Place bones, peeled carrot, onion and celery in a large saucepan and cover with cold water. Bring to the boil: cover and simmer for one hour at least.

2. Meanwhile, mix together lightly beaten egg with minced beef, breadcrumbs and plenty of seasoning.

3. Roll a teaspoon amount into small balls and place on a roasting tin with the oil. Bake in a preheated oven 180°C/350°F/ Gas Mark 3 for 45 minutes, turning occasionally. Strain stock into a saucepan.

4. Push tomatoes and their juice through sieve, and add to stock. Bring to the boil, and simmer for 15 minutes. Add pasta and cook for 10 minutes, stirring frequently.

5. Add meatballs, adjust seasoning, and stir in chopped parsley. Serve hot.

TIME: Preparation takes 10 minutes and cooking takes 1 hour 40 minutes.

MINESTRA

*Some of Italy's finest ingredients
make up this warming soup.*

SERVES 4

1 onion
1 carrot
1 stick celery
2 tbsps olive oil
3 pints water
Salt and pepper
225g/8oz fresh spinach
2 tomatoes
120g/4oz short-cut macaroni
2 cloves garlic, crushed
2 tbsps choped parsley
1 tsp rosemary
60g/2oz Parmesan cheese, grated

1. Cut onion, carrot and celery into thick matchstick strips.

2. Heat oil in a large, heavy pan, and fry vegetable strips until just browning, stirring occasionally. Pour on water, add salt and pepper, and let simmer for 20 minutes.

3. Meanwhile, wash and cut spinach leaves into shreds, add to soup and cook for 10 minutes. Scald and skin tomatoes, and chop roughly, removing seeds.

4. Add tomatoes, macaroni, garlic, parsley and rosemary to the soup, and simmer a further 10 minutes. Adjust seasoning. Serve with grated Parmesan cheese if desired.

TIME: Preparation takes 15 minutes and cooking takes 45 minutes.

MACARONI WITH OLIVE SAUCE

Macaroni is served here with butter, garlic and finely chopped olives.
A very tasty dish that makes an ideal starter.

SERVES 4

300g/11oz macaroni
60g/2oz butter
1 clove garlic, finely chopped
10 olives, green and/or black, finely
   chopped
Salt and pepper

1. Cook the macaroni to your liking in salted, boiling water. Rinse in hot water and set aside to drain.

2. Melt the butter in a saucepan and add the garlic and olives. Cook for 1 minute and then stir in the macaroni.

3. Check the seasoning, adding salt and pepper as necessary. Serve hot.

TIME: Preparation takes about 10 minutes and cooking takes approximately 20 minutes.

VARIATION: Add a few chopped capers to the olives, but reduce the amount of salt.

COOK'S TIP: Rinse the macaroni really well under the water to prevent it from sticking together.

RAVIOLI SOUP

*Fresh pasta rectangles are filled with Parma ham
and butter, then cooked in chicken stock. A tasty and
filling starter for that extra special meal.*

SERVES 4

225g/8oz fresh pasta dough
3 slices Parma ham, cut into very thin strips
30g/1oz butter
1ltr/1¾ pints chicken stock
1 egg, beaten
Nutmeg
Salt and pepper
1 sprig tarragon, leaves stripped off and
    cut into thin strips
2 tbsps single cream

1. Roll the pasta dough very thinly, either with a rolling pin or by passing through a pasta machine, and cut it into rectangles.

2. Place a little Parma ham and butter on one half of each rectangle.

3. Brush the edges of each piece of dough with the beaten egg.

4. Fold each rectangle in half to form a square and pinch the edges well with your fingers to seal. Either trim these squares into various shapes or decorate the edges of the squares with the prongs of a fork.

5. Bring the stock to the boil, and season with nutmeg, salt and pepper.

6. Tip the ravioli into the stock and cook for approximately 2 to 5 minutes, depending on the thickness of the ravioli.

7. Stir the cream into the soup just before serving and sprinkle over the tarragon. Serve hot.

TIME: Preparation takes about 40 minutes (if you have just made the pasta dough, it should rest for 30 minutes in the fridge before rolling) and cooking takes approximately 10 minutes.

COOK'S TIP: The use of cream in the soup is optional, but it gives a nice smooth taste to the stock.

WATCHPOINT: The cooking of the ravioli in the soup should be done on a very gentle simmer – the ravioli may burst open if soup boils vigorously.

VERMICELLI PESCATORE

*This impressive dish is simple to prepare
and perfect for special guests.*

SERVES 4

120g/4oz mussels
120g/4oz cockles
225g/8oz cod fish fillets
120g/4oz squid, cleaned
4 large prawns
4 fresh oysters
2 x 400g/14oz tins plum tomatoes
60ml/4 tbsps olive oil
225ml/8fl oz dry white wine
Half a green pepper, diced
Salt and pepper
300g/10oz vermicelli

1. Prepare seafood. If using fresh mussels, clean closed mussels, removing beard, and cook in boiling water for 3 minutes until they open. (Discard any that remain closed).

2. Cool and remove from shells, keeping a few in shells for garnish if desired. Skin and bone fillets, and cut fish into ½ inch pieces.

3. Clean squid and cut into rings.

4. Force tomatoes and their juice through a sieve, and set aside.

5. Heat 2 tbsps oil in a pan, and add the squid. Fry gently until golden brown, then add wine, tomato purée, green pepper, and salt and pepper to taste. Simmer for 20 minutes then add fish. Simmer for a further 10 minutes, stirring occasionally.

6. Add cockles and mussels and, when mixture reboils, adjust seasoning. Meanwhile, cook vermicelli in lots of boiling salted water for 10 minutes, or until tender but still firm. Drain well. Add seafood, and toss. Garnish with prawns and fresh oyster.

TIME: Preparation takes 15 minutes and cooking takes 40 minutes.

TOMATO SOUP

*A classic soup made extra special
with the addition of macaroni.*

SERVES 4-6

30g/1oz butter or margarine
1 small onion, peeled and chopped
1 small green pepper, cored, seeds
   removed, and chopped
1 tbsp flour
1 ltr/2 pints brown stock, or water plus
   2 beef stock cubes
450g/1lb tomatoes, chopped
2 tbsps tomato purée
120g/4oz short-cut macaroni
1 tbsp grated horseradish
Salt and pepper

Garnish
2 tbsps soured cream
1 tbsp chopped parsley

1. Heat the butter in a pan. Cover and cook the onion and green pepper for 5 minutes. Add the flour and stir.

2. Add stock, tomatoes and tomato purée. Simmer for 15 minutes. Purée soup and pass through a sieve.

3. Return to pan, and season with salt and pepper to taste. Add macaroni 10 minutes before serving. Simmer and stir occasionally. Add horseradish before serving.

4. Garnish with soured cream and parsley. Serve immediately.

TIME: Preparation takes 15 minutes and cooking takes 45 minutes.

CABBAGE AND PASTA SOUP

*Chicken stock flavoured with bacon, cabbage, pasta and
garlic is the base for this light and tasty starter.*

SERVES 4

6 leaves white cabbage
1 tbsp olive oil
150g/5oz small shell pasta
1 rasher streaky bacon, cut into small dice
1 clove garlic, chopped
750ml/1½ pints chicken stock
Salt and pepper

1. Cut the cabbage into thin strips. To do this, roll the leaves into cigar shapes and cut with a very sharp knife.

2. Heat the olive oil and fry the bacon, garlic and cabbage together for 2 minutes.

3. Pour over the stock, season with salt and pepper and cook on a moderate heat for 15 minutes.

4. Add the pasta to the soup and cook for a further 15 minutes.

5. Check the seasoning and serve.

TIME: Preparation takes about 5 minutes and cooking takes approximately 35 minutes.

SERVING IDEA: Sprinkle over a little grated Parmesan cheese just before serving the soup.

VARIATION: Leave the piece of bacon whole and remove before serving the soup.

21

CHICK-PEA SOUP

*This unusual sounding soup is a wonderful mixture
of chick-peas and classic Italian ingredients.*

SERVES 4

150g/5oz dried chick-peas
3 tbsps olive oil
2 cloves garlic
12oz tin plum tomatoes, chopped
1 ltr/1½ pints water
1 tsp basil
1 chicken stock cube
Salt and pepper
120g/4oz soup pasta
2 tbsps Parmesan cheese, grated

1. Soak chick-peas overnight in enough water to cover by 1 inch. Discard water in which the chick-peas have soaked. Place the chick-peas in a large, heavy pan, and cover with 1 inch of water. Bring to the boil and simmer, covered, for about 1 hour until chick-peas are tender, ensuring that they do not boil dry.

2. Heat olive oil in a heavy pan, and sauté garlic cloves. When browned, remove and discard garlic cloves. Add tomatoes and their juice, water and basil, and cook together for 20 minutes.

3. Add drained chick-peas, crumbled stock cube, and salt and pepper to taste. Stir well; simmer a further 10 minutes. Bring back to boil. Add pasta, and cook, stirring frequently, for 10 minutes.

4. Mix in half of the Parmesan cheese. Adjust seasoning, and serve immediately, with remaining Parmesan cheese sprinkled on top.

TIME: Preparation takes overnight soaking for the chick-peas plus 5 minutes and cooking takes 1 hour 20 minutes.

COOK'S NOTE: Soup may be puréed before pasta is added, if desired.

BEAN SOUP

*Kidney beans and pasta combine to produce
a filling soup suitable for all the family.*

SERVES 4-6

430g/15oz tin kidney beans
60g/2oz bacon, rind removed, and
    chopped
1 stick celery, chopped
1 small onion, peeled and chopped
1 clove garlic, crushed
90g/3oz tin plum tomatoes, chopped
    and seeds removed
1 tbsp chopped parsley
1 tsp basil
1 ltr/2 pints water
1 chicken stock cube
Salt and pepper
120g/4oz wholemeal ring pasta

1. Place kidney beans, bacon, celery, onion, garlic, parsley, basil, tomatoes and water in a large pan. Bring to the boil and add stock cube and salt and pepper to taste. Cover and cook over a low heat for about 1½ hours.

2. Raise heat and add pasta, stirring well. Stir frequently until pasta is cooked but still firm – about 10 minutes. Serve immediately.

TIME: Preparation takes 15 minutes and cooking takes 1 hour 45 minutes.

MARINER'S SALAD

*Seafood mixes very well with pasta and the
ingredients can be adapted according to availability.*

SERVES 6

450g/1lb pasta shells, plain and spinach
4 large scallops, cleaned
280ml/½ pint frozen mussels, defrosted
140ml/¼ pint lemon juice and water mixed
120g/4oz shelled and de-veined prawns
140ml/¼ pint cockles or small clams,
     cooked
4 crab sticks, cut in small pieces
4 spring onions, chopped
1 tbsp chopped parsley

Dressing
Grated rind and juice of half a lemon
280ml/½ pint mayonnaise
2 tsps paprika
90ml/3fl oz sour cream or natural yogurt
Salt and pepper

1. Cook the pasta for 10 minutes in a large pan of boiling salted water with 1 tbsp oil. Drain and rinse under hot water. Leave in cold water until ready to use.

2. Cook the scallops and mussels in the lemon juice and water mixture for about 5 minutes or until fairly firm.

3. Cut the scallops into 2 or 3 pieces, depending upon size.

4. Mix the dressing and drain the pasta thoroughly. Mix all ingredients together to coat completely with dressing.

5. Stir carefully so that the shellfish do not break-up. Chill for up to 1 hour before serving.

TIME: Preparation takes 25 minutes and cooking takes 15 minutes.

BEAN SALAD

Bean salad is always popular, and this one is certain to become a favourite with the macaroni and bacon to add to the flavour.

SERVES 4

225g/8oz macaroni
4 strips bacon, diced
1 onion, peeled and chopped
1-2 tbsps wine vinegar
3-4 tbsps olive oil
1 tsp chopped parsley
1 large tin red kidney beans, drained
2 sticks celery, sliced diagonally
Salt
Pepper

1. Cook macaroni in plenty of salted boiling water for 10 minutes, or until tender but still firm. Rinse in cold water and drain well.

2. Heat frying pan, and sauté bacon in its own fat until crisp. Add onion, and cook until soft.

3. Mix vinegar, oil and parsley, and season well.

4. Add bacon, onion, kidney beans, celery and seasoning to macaroni.

5. Pour over dresssing, and toss together.

TIME: Preparation takes 10 minutes and cooking takes 15 minutes.

CURRIED PRAWN SALAD

An unusual salad which is perfect
for a special summer lunch.

SERVES 4

2 tbsps olive oil
1 clove garlic, crushed
1 small onion, peeled and chopped
1½ tsps curry powder
1 tsp paprika
1 tsp tomato purée
140ml/¼ pint water
2 slices lemon
Salt and pepper
1 tsp apricot jam
180ml 6fl oz mayonnaise
225g/8oz soup pasta
225g/8oz prawns, shelled and de-veined
Juice of ½ a lemon

1. Heat oil, and fry garlic and onion gently until soft but not coloured. Add curry powder and paprika, and cook for 2 minutes.

2. Stir in tomato purée and water. Add lemon slices, and salt and pepper to taste. Cook slowly for 10 minutes; stir in jam, and bring to the boil, simmering for 2 minutes. Strain and leave to cool.

3. Add mayonnaise.

4. Meanwhile, cook pasta in plenty of boiling salted water for 10 minutes, or until tender but still firm. Rinse under cold water and drain well. Toss in lemon juice, and put in serving dish. Arrange prawns on top, and pour over curry sauce. Toss well. Sprinkle with paprika.

TIME: Preparation takes 10 minutes and cooking takes 20 minutes.

PASTA AND VEGETABLES IN PARMESAN DRESSING

Fresh vegetables and pasta in a delicious dressing.

SERVES 6

450g/1lb pasta spirals or other shapes
225g/8oz assorted vegetables such as:
Courgettes, cut in rounds or matchsticks
Broccoli, trimmed into very small florets
Mange tout, ends trimmed
Carrots, cut in rounds or matchsticks
Celery, cut in matchsticks
Cucumber, cut in matchsticks
Spring onion, thinly shredded or sliced
Asparagus tips
French beans, sliced
Red or yellow peppers, thinly sliced

Dressing
140ml/¼ pint olive oil
3 tbsps lemon juice
1 tbsp sherry pepper sauce
1 tbsp chopped parsley
1 tbsp chopped basil
60g/2oz freshly grated Parmesan cheese
2 tbsps mild mustard
Salt and pepper
Pinch sugar

1. Cook pasta in a large saucepan of boling salted water with 1 tbsp oil for 10-12 minutes or until just tender. Rinse under hot water to remove starch. Leave in cold water.

2. Place all the vegetables except the cucumber into boiling salted water for 3 minutes until just tender. Rinse in cold water and leave to drain.

3. Mix the dressing ingredients together very well. Drain the pasta thoroughly and toss with the dressing. Add the vegetables and toss to coat. Refrigerate for up to 1 hour before serving.

TIME: Preparation takes 25 minutes and cooking takes 13-15 minutes.

ITALIAN PASTA SALAD

Buy your favourite Italian meats
for this delicious salad.

SERVES 4-6

450g/1lb pasta shapes
120g/4oz peas
225g/8oz assorted Italian meats, cut in strips:
    salami, mortadella, prosciutto, coppa,
    bresaola
120g/4oz provolone or fontina cheese,
    cut in strips
15 black olives, halved and stoned
60g/4 tbsps small capers
1 small red onion or 2 shallots, chopped
150g/6oz oyster mushrooms, stems
    trimmed and sliced

Dressing
3 tbsps white wine vinegar
140ml/¼ pint olive oil
½ clove garlic, minced
1 tsp fennel seed, crushed
1 tbsp chopped parsley
1 tbsp chopped basil
1 tbsp mustard
Salt and pepper

1. Cook the pasta in a large saucepan of boiling water with a pinch of salt and 1 tbsp oil. Cook for about 10 minutes or until just tender.

2. Add the frozen peas during the last 3 minutes of cooking time. Drain the pasta and peas and rinse under hot water. Leave in cold water until ready to use.

3. Mix the dressing ingredients together well.

4. Drain the pasta and peas thoroughly. Mix the pasta and peas with the Italian meats and cheese, olives, capers, chopped onion or shallot and sliced mushrooms.

5. Pour the dressing over the salad and toss all the ingredients together to coat. Do not over-mix.

6. Leave the salad to chill for up to 1 hour before serving.

TIME: Preparation takes 25 minutes and cooking takes 10 minutes.

Niçoise Salad

A classic French salad using
Italy's favourite ingredients!

SERVES 4

225g/8oz penne
200g/7oz can tuna fish, drained
   and flaked
3 tomatoes, quartered
½ cucumber, cut into batons
120g/4oz French beans, cooked
12 black olives, halved, with stones
   removed
45g/1½ oz can anchovy fillets, drained,
   and soaked in milk if desired
120ml/4fl oz bottled French dressing

1. Cook penne in lots of boiling salted water until tender but still firm.

2. Rinse in cold water; drain, and leave to dry.

3. Put flaked tuna in the base of a salad dish. Toss pasta together with tomatoes, cucumber, French beans, olives, and anchovies, and the pour over French dressing. Mix together well.

TIME: Preparation takes 15 minutes and cooking takes 15 minutes.

TUNA AND TOMATO SALAD

An economical salad which uses few
ingredients – perfect for unexpected guests.

SERVES 4

1 tbsp fresh chopped basil or marjoram,
　or 1 tsp dried basil or oregano
90ml/6 tbsps French dressing
225g/8oz pasta shells
200g/7oz can tuna fish, flaked
6 tomatoes

1. Mix herbs with French dressing.

2. Cook pasta shells in a large saucepan of boiling salted water until tender – about 10 minutes. Rinse with cold water, and drain, shaking off excess water. Toss with 3 tablespoons of French dressing. Leave to cool.

3. Meanwhile, slice enough of the tomatoes to arrange around the outside of the serving-dish.

4. Chop the rest, and pour the remaining French dressing over them, and place in the centre of the dish.

5. Add tuna to the pasta shells, and toss gently. Serve in the centre of the dish over the chopped tomatoes.

TIME: Preparation takes 10 minutes and cooking takes 15 minutes.

MEXICAN CHICKEN SALAD

A simple salad which is both quick and tasty.

SERVES 4

225g/8oz soup pasta shells
225g/8oz cooked chicken, shredded
200g/7oz can sweetcorn kernels, drained
1 stick celery, sliced
1 red pepper, cored, seeds removed, and
   diced
1 green pepper, cored, seeds removed,
   and diced

Dressing
1 tbsp mayonnaise
2 tbsps vinegar
Salt
Pepper

1. Cook pasta in plenty of boiling salted water until just tender. Drain well, and leave to cool.

2. Meanwhile, combine mayonnaise with vinegar and salt and pepper to taste.

3. When the pasta is cooked, add chicken, sweetcorn, celery and peppers.

4. Toss together well and serve with the dressing.

TIME: Preparation takes 10 minutes and cooking takes 15 minutes.

GIANFOTTERE SALAD

*Aubergines, courgettes and peppers are
combined with pasta in this simple salad.*

SERVES 4

1 aubergine
2 tomatoes
1 courgette
1 red pepper
1 green pepper
1 onion
60ml/4 tbsps olive oil
1 clove garlic
Salt and pepper
225g/8oz pasta spirals

1. Cut aubergine into 1 cm/½ inch slices. Sprinkle with salt and leave for 30 minutes.

2. Skin the tomatoes by putting them into boiling water for 20 seconds, and then rinsing in cold water, and peeling skins off. Chop roughly.

3. Cut courgette into 1cm/½ inch slices. Remove cores and seeds from the peppers, and chop roughly.

4. Peel and chop onion.

5. Heat 3 tbsps olive oil in pan, and fry onion gently until transparent.

6. Meanwhile, rinse salt from aubergine, and pat dry with absorbent paper. Chop roughly.

7. Add aubergine, courgette, peppers, tomatoes and garlic to onion, and fry gently for 20 minutes. Season with salt and pepper. Allow to cool.

8. Meanwhile, cook pasta spirals in a lot of boiling salted water for 10 minutes, or until tender but still firm. Rinse in cold water and drain well, and toss in remaining 1 tbsp olive oil.

9. Toss vegetables together with pasta spirals.

TIME: Preparation takes 40 minutes and cooking takes 30 minutes.

MUSHROOM PASTA SALAD

Mushrooms are always delicious in a salad and this recipe, which combines them with wholemeal pasta shapes, is no exception.

SERVES 4

75ml/5 tbsps olive oil
Juice of 2 lemons
1 tsp fresh chopped basil
1 tsp fresh chopped parsley
Salt and freshly ground black pepper
225g/8oz mushrooms
225g/8oz wholemeal pasta shapes, of your
   choice

1. In a large bowl mix together the olive oil, lemon juice, herbs and seasoning.

2. Finely slice the mushrooms and add these to the lemon dressing in the bowl, stirring well to coat the mushrooms evenly.

3. Cover the bowl with cling film and allow to stand in a cool place for at least 1 hour.

4. Put the pasta into a large saucepan and cover with boiling water. Season with a little salt and simmer for 10 minutes, or until just tender.

5. Rinse the pasta in cold water and drain well.

6. Add the pasta to the marinated mushrooms and lemon dressing, mixing well to coat evenly.

7. Adjust the seasoning if necessary, then chill well before serving.

TIME: Preparation takes approximately 10 minutes, plus 1 hour at least for the mushrooms to marinate. Cooking takes about 15 minutes.

VARIATION: Use a mixture of button and wild mushrooms for a delicious variation in flavour.

SERVING IDEA: Serve mushroom pasta salad on a bed of mixed lettuce.

Courgette Salad

*Raw vegetables are full of vitamins, and raw courgette in
particular has the added advantage of having a delicious taste and texture.*

SERVES 4

225g/8oz macaroni
4 tomatoes
4-5 courgettes, sliced thinly
8 stuffed green olives, sliced
90ml/6 tbsps French dressing

1. Put the macaroni into a large saucepan and cover with boiling water. Add a little salt and simmer for 10 minutes, or until tender but still firm. Rinse in cold water and drain well.

2. Cut a small cross in the tops of each tomato and plunge into boiling water for 30 seconds.

3. Carefully remove the skins from the blanched tomatoes, using a sharp knife. Chop the tomatoes coarsely.

4. Mix all the ingredients in a large bowl and chill in the refrigerator for 30 minutes before serving.

TIME: Preparation takes 15 minutes and cooking takes about 10 minutes.

VARIATION: Use any other pasta shape of your choice.

TUNA AND PASTA WITH RED KIDNEY BEANS

The perfect summer salad for lunch or a light dinner.

SERVES 4-6

225g/8oz small pasta shells
225g/8oz tin red kidney beans,
   drained and rinsed
120g/4oz small mushrooms, quartered
1 can tuna, drained and flaked
4 spring onions, sliced
2 tbsps chopped mixed herbs

Dressing
140ml/¼ pint olive oil
3 tbsps white wine vinegar
Squeeze lemon juice
1 tbsp Dijon mustard
Salt and pepper

1. Cook the pasta shells in boiling salted water with 1 tbsp oil for 10 minutes or until just tender. Rinse under hot water and then place in cold water until ready to use.

2. Mix the dressing ingredients together thoroughly.

3. Drain the pasta shells. Mix the pasta with the beans, mushrooms, tuna, spring onions and chopped mixed herbs.

4. Pour over the dressing and toss to coat. Chill up to 1 hour in the refrigerator before serving.

TIME: Preparation takes 20 minutes and cooking takes 10 minutes.

Spaghetti Amatriciana

This is another quickly cooked sauce with a rich spicy taste.
Use less of the chilli pepper for a less fiery flavour.

SERVES 4

1 onion
6 strips smoked back bacon
450g/1lb ripe tomatoes
1 red chilli pepper
25ml/1½ tbsps oil
340g/12oz spaghetti

1. Slice the onion thinly. Remove rind from the bacon and cut into thin strips.

2. Drop the tomatoes into boiling water for 6-8 seconds. Remove with a draining spoon, place in cold water, and leave to cool completely. This will make the peels easier to remove.

3. When the tomatoes are peeled, cut them in half and remove the seeds and pulp with a teaspoon. Rub the seeds and pulp through a strainer and retain juice to use in the sauce if desired. Chop the tomato flesh roughly and set it aside.

4. Cut the stem off the chilli pepper and cut the pepper in half lengthways. Remove the seeds and core and cut the pepper into thin strips. Cut the strips into small dice.

5. Heat the oil in a sauté pan and add the onion and bacon. Stir over medium heat for about 5 minutes, until the onion is transparent. Drain off excess fat and add the tomatoes and chilli and mix well. Simmer the sauce gently, uncovered, for about 5 minutes, stirring occasionally.

6. Meanwhile, cook the spaghetti in boiling salted water with 1 tbsp oil for about 10-12 minutes. Drain and rinse in hot water and toss in a colander to dry. To serve, spoon the sauce on top of the spaghetti and sprinkle with freshly grated Parmesan cheese, if desired.

TIME: Preparation takes about 20-25 minutes and cooking takes about 10-12 minutes for the spaghetti and about 8 minutes for the sauce.

PASTA SPIRALS WITH CREAMY PARSLEY SAUCE

*Serve this quick and easy dish with crusty
bread for the perfect mid-week dinner.*

SERVES 3-4

2 tbsps butter or margarine
1 tbsp flour
280ml/½ pint milk
250g/9oz package pasta spirals
1 tbsp chopped parsley
1 tbsp lemon juice, or 1 tsp vinegar

1. Heat butter in pan; when melted, stir in flour. Heat gently for 1 minute. Remove from heat, and gradually stir in milk. Return to heat, and stir continuously until boiling. Cook for 2 minutes.

2. Meanwhile, cook pasta spirals in lots of boiling salted water for 10 minutes, or until tender but still firm. Rinse in hot water, and drain well.

3. Just before serving, add parsley and lemon juice to sauce, and pour over pasta. Serve immediately.

TIME: Preparation takes 5 minutes and cooking takes 15 minutes.

TORTIGLIONI ALLA PUTTANESCA

*Anchovy fillets add a special flavour
to this classic Italian dish.*

SERVES 4

200g/7oz can plum tomatoes, drained
45g/1½ oz tin anchovy fillets, drained
300g/10oz tortiglioni, spiral pasta
2 tbsps olive oil
2 cloves garlic, crushed
½ tsp basil
Pinch chilli powder
120g/4oz black olives, stoned and
　　chopped
2 tbsps chopped parsley
Salt and pepper

1. Chop tomatoes and remove seeds, and chop anchovies.

2. Cook pasta in plenty of boiling salted water for 10 minutes, or until tender but still firm. Rinse in hot water, and drain. Pour into a warmed bowl.

3. Meanwhile, heat oil in pan, add garlic, basil and chilli powder and cook for 1 minute.

4. Add tomatoes, olives, parsley and anchovies, and cook for a few minutes. Season with salt and pepper. Pour sauce over pasta, and mix together thoroughly. Serve immediately.

TIME: Preparation takes 10 minutes and cooking takes 15 minutes.

Pasta Shells with Mushroom Sauce

This adaptable dish can be served for lunch or dinner.

SERVES 3-4

225g/8oz mushrooms
30g/1oz butter or margarine
1 tbsp flour
420ml/¾ pint milk
Salt and pepper
300g/10oz package pasta shells

1. Rinse the mushrooms and chop them roughly.

2. Melt butter in a saucepan and add mushrooms. Fry for 5 minutes, stirring occasionally. Stir in the flour and cook for 1 minute.

3. Reduce the heat, and add milk gradually, stirring continuously. Bring to the boil and cook for 3 minutes. Season with salt and pepper.

4. Meanwhile, cook the pasta shells in lots of boiling salted water for 10 minutes, or until tender but still firm.

5. Rinse in hot water and drain well. Place in a warmed serving dish, and pour over mushroom sauce. Serve immediately.

TIME: Preparation takes 5 minutes and cooking takes 15 minutes.

TAGLIATELLE WITH CREAMY LIVER SAUCE

Chicken livers are lovely mixed with cream and mushrooms,
add pasta to the mixture and you have the perfect mid-week treat.

SERVES 3-4

45ml/3 tbsps olive oil
2 medium onions, peeled and sliced
1 clove garlic, crushed
120g/4oz mushrooms, sliced
450g/1lb chicken livers, cleaned and sliced
120ml/4fl oz single cream
2 eggs, beaten
Salt and pepper
300g/10oz tagliatelle
1 tbsp chopped parsley

1. Melt 2 tbsps of the oil in a large frying pan and cook onions and garlic gently until softened.

2. Add mushrooms and cook for 3 minutes. Add chicken livers to onions and mushrooms, and cook until lightly browned. Remove from heat and stir in cream. Return to low heat, and cook, uncovered, for a further 2 minutes.

3. Remove from heat and stir in lightly beaten eggs. Season with salt and pepper to taste.

4. Meanwhile, cook the tagliatelle in plenty of boiling salted water for 10 minutes, or until tender but still firm, stirring occasionally.

5. Drain tagliatelle, toss in remaining oil, and black pepper. Serve sauce over tagliatelle and sprinkle with parsley.

TIME: Preparation takes 10 minutes and cooking takes 15 minutes.

LASAGNE ROLLS

*An interesting and simple way
to use sheets of lasagne.*

SERVES 4

---

2 tsps olive oil
8 lasagne sheets
60g/2oz button mushrooms, sliced
225g/8oz boned chicken breasts
2 tbsps butter or margarine
1 tbsp flour
140ml/¼ pint milk
120g/4oz Gruyère or Cheddar cheese,
   grated
Salt and pepper

---

1. In a large saucepan, fill two-thirds with boiling salted water and 2 teaspoons oil. Bring to the boil. Add 1 sheet of lasagne; wait about 2 minutes, and add another sheet. Only cook a few at a time. When tender, remove, and rinse under cold water, and leave to drain. Repeat until all the lasagne is cooked.

2. Meanwhile, wash and slice mushrooms, and slice chicken. Put half the butter in a small frying pan, and fry the mushrooms and chicken.

3. In a small saucepan, melt the rest of the butter.

4. Add the flour, and cook for a minute. Remove from the heat, and add the milk. Mix well and bring to the boil. Cook for 3 minutes.

5. Add sauce to chicken and mushrooms, and add half the cheese, mixing well. Add salt and pepper to taste.

6. Spread out lasagne, and spread one-eighth mixture at one end of each. Roll up each piece of lasagne, and put into an oven-proof dish. Sprinkle with remaining cheese, and put under a grill until golden brown. Serve immediately.

TIME: Preparation takes 5 minutes and cooking takes 15 minutes.

SPAGHETTI WITH TOMATO, SALAMI AND GREEN OLIVES

*Vary the quantities of salami and green olives
in this recipe according to your taste.*

SERVES 2-3

400g/14oz tin plum tomatoes
150g/5oz salami, sliced and shredded
200g/7oz green olives, stoned and
   chopped
½ tbsp oregano
Salt and pepper
300g/10oz spaghetti
2 tbsps olive oil
1 clove garlic, crushed
60g/2oz pecorino cheese, grated

1. Purée tomatoes, and push through a sieve into a saucepan. Add oregano, olives and salami and heat gently. Add salt and pepper to taste.

2. Meanwhile, cook spaghetti in plenty of boiling salted water for 10 minutes, or until tender but still firm. Drain well.

3. Heat olive oil, add garlic and freshly-ground black pepper to the pan used to cook the spaghetti.

4. Add spaghetti, and pour the sauce over. Toss well. Serve immediately with pecorino cheese.

TIME: Preparation takes 15 minutes and cooking takes 15 minutes.

MACARONI CHEESE WITH FRANKFURTERS

Kids and adults alike will love this delicious, filling meal.

SERVES 4

8 Frankfurter sausages, or 400g/14oz tin
   hot-dog sausages
225g/8oz macaroni
60g/2oz butter or margarine
60g/2oz flour
570ml/1 pint milk
175g/6oz Cheddar cheese, grated
1 tsp dry mustard
Salt and pepper

Garnish
½ red pepper, cut into thin strips

1. Poach the Frankfurter sausages for 5-8 minutes. Remove skins and, when cold, cut into diagonal slices. (If using hot-dog sausages, just cut as required).

2. Cook macaroni in plenty of boiling salted water for about 10 minutes, or until tender but still firm. Rinse in hot water, and drain well.

3. Meanwhile, melt the butter in a pan. Stir in the flour, and cook gently for 1 minute. Reduce heat, and gradually add milk, stirring all the time. Bring to the boil, stirring continuously, reduce heat and cook gently for 3 minutes.

4. Add sausages, grated cheese, mustard, and salt and pepper to taste. Stir well.

5. Add macaroni, and mix in well. Pour mixture into an oven-proof dish, and sprinkle the remaining cheese over the top.

6. Make a lattice of pepper, and cook under a preheated grill until golden brown. Serve immediately.

TIME: Preparation takes 10 minutes and cooking takes 20 minutes.

SPIRALI WITH SPINACH AND BACON

Pasta doesn't have to have a sauce that cooks for hours. This whole dish takes about 15 minutes. True Italian 'fast food'!

SERVES 4

340g/12oz pasta spirals
225g/8oz fresh spinach
90g/3oz bacon
1 small red or green chilli pepper
1 small red pepper
1 small onion
1 clove garlic, crushed
3 tbsps olive oil
Salt and pepper

1. Cook the pasta in boiling salted water for about 10-12 minutes or until just tender. Drain the pasta in a colander and rinse it under hot water. Keep the pasta in a bowl of water until ready to use.

2. Tear the stalks off the spinach and wash the leaves well in the water several times. Set aside to drain.

3. Remove the rind and bones from the bacon, if necessary, and dice the bacon finely. Cut the chilli and the red pepper in half, remove the stems, core and seed and slice finely. Slice the onion thinly.

4. Roll up several of the spinach leaves into a cigar shape and then shred them finely. Repeat until all the spinach is shredded.

5. Heat the oil in a sauté pan and add garlic, onion, peppers and bacon. Fry for 2 minutes, add the spinach and fry for a further 2 minutes, stirring continuously. Season with salt and pepper.

6. Drain the pasta spirals and toss them in a colander to remove excess water. Mix with the spinach sauce and serve immediately.

TIME: Preparation takes about 15 minutes.

Penne with Ham and Asparagus

*The Italian word penne means quills, due to the
diagonal cut on both ends.*

SERVES 4

225g/8oz penne
430g/12oz fresh asparagus
120g/4oz cooked ham
2 tbsps butter or margarine
280ml/½ pint double cream

---

1. Using a swivel vegetable peeler, scrape the sides of the asparagus spears starting about 5cm/2 inches from the top. Cut off the ends of the spears about 2.5cm/1 inch from the bottom.

2. Cut the ham into strips about 1.25cm/½ inch thick.

3. Bring a sauté pan of water to the boil, adding a pinch of salt. Move the pan so it is half on and half off direct heat. Place in the asparagus spears so that the tips are off the heat. Cover the pan and bring back to the boil. Cook the asparagus spears for about 2 minutes. Drain and allow to cool.

4. Cut the asparagus into 2.5cm/1 inch lengths, leaving the tips whole.

5. Melt the butter in the sauté pan and add the asparagus and ham. Cook briefly to evaporate the liquid, and add the cream. Bring to the boil and cook for about 5 minutes to thicken the cream.

6. Meanwhile, cook the pasta in boiling salted water with 1 tbsp oil for about 10-12 minutes.

7. Drain the pasta and rinse under hot water. Toss in a colander to drain and mix with the sauce. Serve with grated Parmesan cheese, if desired.

TIME: Preparation takes about 20 minutes and cooking takes
10-12 minutes for the pasta and 8 minutes for the sauce.

HOME-MADE TAGLIATELLE WITH SUMMER SAUCE

Pasta making is not as difficult as you might think. It is well worth it, too, because home-made pasta is in a class by itself.

SERVES 4

Pasta Dough

120g/4oz plain flour
120g/4oz fine semolina
2 large eggs
2 tsps olive oil
Pinch salt

Sauce

450g/1lb unpeeled tomatoes, seeded and
 cut into small dice
1 large green pepper, cored, seeded and
 cut in small dice
1 onion, cut in small dice
1 tbsp chopped fresh basil
1 tbsp chopped fresh parsley
2 cloves garlic, crushed
140ml/¼ pint olive oil and vegetable oil
 mixed

1. Combine all the sauce ingredients, mixing well. Cover and refrigerate overnight.

2. Place the flours in a mound on a work surface and make a well in the centre. Place the eggs, oil and salt in the centre of the well.

3. Using a fork, beat the ingredients in the centre to blend them and gradually incorporate the flour from the outside edge. The dough may also be mixed in a food processor.

4. When half the flour is incorporated, start kneading using the palms of the hands and not the fingers until all the flour is incorporated. This may also be done in a food processor. Cover the dough and leave it to rest for 15 minutes.

5. Divide the dough in quarters and roll out thinly with a rolling pin on a floured surface or use a pasta machine, dusting dough lightly with flour before rolling. If using a machine, following the manufacturer's directions. Allow the sheets of pasta to dry for about 10 minutes on a floured surface or tea towels. Cut the sheets into strips about 5mm/¼ inch wide by hand or machine, dusting lightly with flour while cutting. Leave the cut pasta to dry for 5-10 minutes.

6. Cook the pasta for 5-6 minutes in boiling salted water with a spoonful of oil. Drain the pasta and rinse under very hot water. Toss in a colander to drain excess water. Place the hot pasta in serving dish. Pour the cold sauce over and toss.

TIME: Preparation takes about 30 minutes and cooking takes about 5-6 minutes.

PASTA WITH FRESH TOMATO AND BASIL SAUCE

Pasta is a good item to include on a low calorie diet, as it is very filling and can be served with any variety of low calorie sauces.

SERVES 4-6

1 small onion, finely chopped
450g/1lb fresh tomatoes
2 tbsps tomato purée
1 orange
2 cloves garlic, crushed
Salt and freshly ground black pepper
140ml/¼ pint red wine
140ml/¼ pint chicken stock
2 tbsps coarsely chopped basil
340g/12oz wholemeal pasta

1. Peel and finely chop the onion.

2. Cut a small cross in the skins of the tomatoes and plunge them into boiling water for 30 seconds. Remove the blanched tomatoes from the water and carefully peel away the loosened skin.

3. Cut the tomatoes into quarters, and remove and discard the pips. Chop the tomato flesh roughly, and put this, the onion and the tomato purée into a large saucepan.

4. Heat the onion and tomatoes over a gentle heat, stirring continuously until the tomatoes soften and begin to lose their juice.

5. Finely grate the rind from the orange. Cut the orange in half and squeeze out the juice.

6. Put the orange, rind and juice into a large saucepan along with all the remaining ingredients except the pasta, and bring to the boil.

7. Continue to boil until the sauce has reduced and thickened and the vegetables are soft.

8. Whilst the sauce is cooking, put the pasta into another saucepan with enough boiling water to cover. Season with a little salt and cook for 10-15 minutes, or until the pasta is soft.

9. Drain the pasta in a colander, and stir it into the hot sauce.

10. Serve at once with salad.

TIME: Preparation takes 15-20 minutes, cooking takes 10-15 minutes.

VARIATION: Add 120g/4oz thinly sliced mushrooms to the sauce.

NOODLES WITH POPPY SEEDS AND RAISINS

*Pasta is not just a favourite in Italy,
this is a traditional Polish dish.*

SERVES 6

225g/8oz noodles or other pasta shapes
Pinch salt
1 tbsp oil
140ml/¼ pint double cream
90g/6 tbsps black poppy seeds, ground
2 tbsps honey
90g/6 tbsps raisins

1. Bring lots of water to the boil in a large saucepan with a pinch of salt. Add the oil and the noodles or other pasta shapes and bring back to the boil. Cook, uncovered, until tender, about 10-12 minutes.

2. Drain and rinse the pasta under hot water. If using immediately, allow to drain dry. If not, place in a bowl of hot water to keep.

3. Place the cream in a deep, heavy-based saucepan and bring almost to the boil. When the cream reaches the scalding point, mix in the poppy seeds, honey and raisins. Cook slowly for about 5 minutes. The mixture should become thick but still fall off a spoon easily. Use a food processor or spice mill to grind the poppy seeds.

4. Toss the poppy seed mixture with the noodles and serve hot.

TIME: Preparation takes about 15 minutes and cooking takes 15-17 minutes.

LASAGNE WITH FOUR CHEESES

Adapt this dish by using your own
favourite Italian cheeses.

SERVES 2-3

1 tbsp olive oil
225g/½ lb green lasagne
½ stick butter
3 tbsps plain flour
700ml/1¼ pints milk
90g/3oz grated Parmesan cheese
60g/2oz grated gruyére cheese
60g/2oz mozzarella, diced
60g/2oz pecorino, diced
Salt, pepper and nutmeg

1. Fill a large pan with salted water. Add the olive oil. Cook the lasagne 4 or 5 sheets at a time for 7-10 minutes. Lift each batch out carefully, plunge into cold water. When all the pasta has been cooked, drain well on absorbent paper.

2. Melt the butter over gentle heat. When melted, add the flour and mix well. Heat the mixture gently until it turns a pale straw colour. Stir in the milk gradually stirring constantly until thick. Add the cheeses to the sauce, reserving 2 tbsps Parmesan. Season with salt, pepper and nutmeg.

3. Stir until cheeses have melted.

4. Butter a deep baking pan generously. Add alternate layers of lasagne and sauce – there should be at least four layers. Finish with a layer of sauce, sprinkle with the reserved grated Parmesan. Cook at 180°C/ 350°F/Gas Mark 4 for 45 minutes until bubbling and golden brown.

TIME: Preparation takes 15-20 minutes and cooking takes 45 minutes.

MEAT RAVIOLI WITH RED PEPPER SAUCE

Pepper-flavoured pasta dough is rolled thinly, cut into squares, filled with a delicious meat stuffing and served with a creamy red pepper sauce.

SERVES 4

2 red peppers, seeded
200g/7oz flour, sifted
2 eggs
200g/7oz minced beef
1 tbsp finely chopped parsley
½ onion, chopped
120ml/4 fl oz single cream
90g/3oz butter
Salt and pepper

1. Place the red peppers in a food processor and blend until liquid. Place in a small bowl and set aside, giving time for the pulp to rise to the surface. This takes approximately 30 minutes.

2. To make the dough, place the sifted flour in a bowl with a pinch of salt. Add 1 egg and 3 tbsps of the pepper pulp (not the juice).

3. Mix together really well and form into a ball. Set the dough aside for 30 minutes.

4. Mix together the meat, parsley and onion and season with salt and pepper.

5. Roll the dough out very thinly, using a pasta machine if available, and cut into small squares. Place a little stuffing on half of the cut squares. Beat the remaining egg and brush the edges of the squares with the egg. Cover with another square of dough and seal the edges by pinching together with your fingers.

6. Bring a large saucepan of salted water to boil and cook the ravioli for approximately 3 minutes – longer if you prefer your pasta well cooked.

7. While the ravioli are cooking, prepare the sauce by heating the cream with 120ml/4fl oz of the red pepper pulp. Bring to the boil and then whisk in the butter.

8. Drain the ravioli and then pat them dry with a tea towel. Serve with the hot cream sauce.

TIME: Preparation takes about 50 minutes, resting time 30 minutes and cooking time approximately 15 minutes.

VARIATION: Add a little wine vinegar (1 tsp) and a few drops of Tabasco to the sauce to give it a slightly peppery taste.

WATCHPOINT: When rolling out the dough, flour it well so that it does not stick to the rolling pin or pasta machine rollers.

SPAGHETTI WITH CRAB AND BACON

This recipe includes a wonderful preparation of home-made parsley pasta.
It is tossed and served with a seafood sauce, crab and bacon.

SERVES 6

1 bunch parsley (approximately 6 tbsps)
500g/1lb 2oz flour
4 eggs
225g/8oz bacon, in one piece
1 tbsp olive oil
10 crab sticks
370ml/13fl oz double cream
3 tbps butter
Fresh chervil
Salt and pepper

1. Trim the leaves off the parsley, discard the stalks. Cook for 10 minutes in boiling water. Pass through a fine sieve and reserve the cooking liquid.

2. Purée the parsley with 3 tbsps of the cooking liquid in a blender.

3. In a bowl, mix together the flour, salt, eggs and 1½ tbsps parsley purée. Form into a ball.

4. Quarter the dough and form these pieces into balls. Press each ball flat and run it through a pasta machine.

5. Thin the dough progressively by passing it through the machine several times. Flour the dough frequently through the operation.

6. Run the flattened strips of dough through the spaghetti cutter.

7. Cut the rind off the bacon and cut the bacon first into strips, and then into small rectangles.

8. Add the olive oil to boiling, salted water and cook the spaghetti for 5 minutes. Strain and rinse.

9. Break up the crab sticks with your fingers.

10. Heat the cream gently with the crab and bacon pieces.

11. Meanwhile, heat the butter in a pan and when it bubbles, add the spaghetti (first reheat by plunging for 30 seconds in boiling water). Mix well and season with salt and pepper.

12. Place the buttered spaghetti around the edges of the dinner plates and arrange the crab/bacon mixture in the centre. Garnish with chopped fresh herbs.

TIME: Preparation takes 1 hour and cooking takes 20 minutes.

COOK'S TIP: If you do not wish to prepare the spaghetti yourself you can buy fresh spaghetti, either parsley or plain verde at a delicatessen or supermarket.

TAGLIATELLE WITH BLUE CHEESE

Fruit and cheese marries well to give a sweet and savoury dish.

SERVES 6

500g/1lb 2oz flour
5 eggs
1 tbsp olive oil
120g/4oz blue cheese (roquefort or stilton)
150g/5oz dried apricots
280ml/½ pint double cream
120ml/4fl oz milk
30g/1oz pine nuts
½ bunch chives
Salt and pepper

---

1. In a bowl, work together the flour, a pinch of salt and eggs to form a soft ball of dough.

2. Quarter the dough and flatten each piece. Dredge each piece with plenty of flour. Flour the rollers of a pasta machine, and either pass the dough through the machine or roll it out with a rolling pin.

3. Continue rolling the pasta until thin. Flour frequently during the process.

4. Thread the dough strips through the tagliatelle cutter, or cut into strips with a knife. Dredge the noodles with flour and allow to dry for 2 hours.

5. Bring to the boil a saucepan of salted water with 1 tbsp oil. Cook the pasta for 2 to 4 minutes, stirring with a fork.

6. Drain the tagliatelle and rinse in plenty of cold water to prevent sticking. Set aside.

7. Break up the cheese and force through a sieve with the back of a spoon.

8. Cut the apricots into strips then dice.

9. Slowly heat the cream in a saucepan. Stir in the cheese and milk. Blend until smooth with a hand-held electric blender.

10. Whilst the sauce is hot, stir in the tagliatelle and apricots, and season as necessary. Heat through quickly, so the cream does not curdle, or the noodles overcook.

11. Mix the pasta with two forks. Remove from the heat, and mix in the pine nuts.

12. Chop the chives finely and sprinkle them over the tagliatelle; serve immediately.

TIME: Preparation takes 1 hour and cooking takes 16 minutes. Drying takes 2 hours.

Pasta with Leeks and Mussels

*An easy pasta dish to prepare, ideal
for when you have unexpected guests.*

SERVES 6

20-25 mussels
120ml/4fl oz white wine
1 shallot, choped
2 medium-sized leeks
200ml/7fl oz double cream
450g/1lb pasta spirals
1 tbsp oil
2 slices ham
1½ tbsps butter
Fresh chives to garnish
Salt and pepper

1. Scrub the mussels; remove the beards and wash in several changes of water to remove any sand.

2. In a large, covered saucepan, cook the mussels in the white wine with the chopped shallot for approximately 5 minutes, over a high heat.

3. Cool, and remove the opened mussels from their shells. Reserve the cooking liquid.

4. Quarter each leek lengthwise, wash thoroughly, and slice finely.

5. In a covered saucepan, cook the leeks in the cream, with salt and pepper to taste, for 10 minutes over a low heat.

6. In a large casserole of water, boil the pasta with 1 tbsp oil. Stir the pasta as it cooks, to prevent sticking.

7. Drain after 5 or 6 minutes. Rinse in cold water to prevent sticking.

8. Remove any fat or rind from the ham, and slice into small pieces.

9. Strain the mussel cooking liquid through a sieve lined with cheesecloth. Measure out approximately ½ cup.

10. Add the shelled mussels and the mussel liquid to the cream mixture, and cook for 4 minutes, stirring constantly.

11. Melt the butter in a deep frying pan, and reheat the pasta gently with the ham. Season to taste.

12. When the pasta is heated through, add the cream and leek sauce, and serve garnished with the chopped chives.

TIME: Preparation takes 30 minutes and cooking takes 25 minutes.

FISH RAVIOLI

This recipe has quite a few ingredients but it is not too difficult to prepare and the end result tastes wonderful.

SERVES 4

Dough
275g/9oz strong bread flour
Pinch of salt
3 eggs

Filling
225g/8oz sole fillets, or flounder, skinned
 and boned
1 slice of onion
1 slice of lemon
6 peppercorns
1 bay leaf
1 tbsp lemon juice
280ml/½ pint water
2 eggs, beaten
2 tbsps breadcrumbs
1 spring onion, finely chopped

Lemon sauce
2 tbsps butter or margarine
2 tbsps flour
280ml/½ pint strained cooking liquid from
 fish
2 tbsps double cream
2 tbsps lemon juice
Salt and pepper

Filling
1. Preheat oven to 180°C/350°F/Gas Mark 4.

2. Wash and dry fish. Place in oven-proof dish with slice of onion, slice of lemon, peppercorns, bay leaf, lemon juice and water. Cover and cook for 20 minutes.

3. Remove fish from liquid, and allow to drain. Strain liquid, and set aside. When fish is cool, beat with the back of a spoon to a pulp.

4. Add eggs, breadcrumbs and spring onion, and salt and pepper to taste. Mix well.

Dough
1. Sift flour and salt into a bowl. Make a well in the centre, and add the eggs. Work the flour and eggs together with a spoon, and then knead by hand, until a smooth dough is formed. Leave to rest for 15 minutes.

2. Lightly flour a board, roll out dough thinly into a rectangle and cut in half.

3. Shape the filling into small balls, and set them about 1½ inches apart on one half of the dough. Place the other half of the dough on top, and cut with a ravioli cutter or small pastry cutter. Seal the edges.

4. Cook in batches in a large, wide pan with plenty of boiling salted water until tender – about 8 minutes. Remove carefully with a perforated spoon. Meanwhile, make the sauce.

Sauce
1. Melt butter in pan. Stir in flour, and cook gently for 30 seconds. Reduce the heat, and gradually stir in liquid from cooked fish. Return to heat and bring to the boil. Simmer for 4 minutes, stirring continuously.

2. Add cream and mix well. Season to taste. Remove from heat, and gradually stir in lemon juice and seasoning. Do not reboil. Pour sauce over ravioli and serve immediately.

TIME: Preparation takes 30 minutes and cooking takes 30 minutes.

PASTITSIO

This is like an Italian version of Shepherd's Pie with
tomatoes in the mince and macaroni instead of potato.

SERVES 4

225g/8oz package macaroni
90g/3oz butter or margarine
60g/2oz Parmesan cheese, grated
Pinch of grated nutmeg
2 eggs, beaten
1 medium onion, peeled and chopped
1 clove garlic, crushed
450g/1lb minced beef
2 tbsps tomato purée
60ml/2fl oz red wine
90ml/3fl oz beef stock
2 tbsps chopped parsley
2 tbsps plain flour
280ml/½ pint milk
Salt
Pepper

1. Preheat oven to 190°C/375°F/Gas Mark 5.

2. Cook macaroni in plenty of boiling salted water for 10 minutes, or until tender but still firm. Rinse under hot water. Drain.

3. Put one-third of the butter in the pan and return macaroni to it. Add half the cheese, nutmeg, and salt and pepper to taste. Leave to cool. Mix in half the beaten egg, and put aside.

4. Melt half of the remaining butter in a pan, and fry the onion and garlic gently until onion is soft. Increase temperature, add meat, and fry until browned.

5. Add tomato purée, stock, parsley and wine, and season with salt and pepper. Simmer for 20 minutes.

6. In a small pan, melt the rest of the butter. Stir in the flour and cook for 30 seconds. Remove from heat, and stir in milk. Bring to boil, stirring continuously, until the sauce thickens.

7. Beat in the remaining egg and season to taste. Spoon half the macaroni into a serving dish and cover with the meat sauce.

8. Put on another layer of macaroni and smooth over. Pour over white sauce, sprinkle with remaining cheese, and bake in the oven for 30 minutes until golden brown. Serve immediately.

TIME: Preparation takes 10 minutes and cooking takes 1 hour.

SALMON AND FENNEL LASAGNE

Thin strips of pasta are pre-cooked and then layered with salmon and bechamel sauce. Fish stock is poured over and the dish is then topped with cheese and cooked in the oven. Absolutely mouthwatering!

SERVES 4

350g/12oz flour, sifted
3 eggs, beaten
225ml/8fl oz fairly runny white sauce (see recipe for Pasta Spirals with Creamy Parsley Sauce)
600g/1⅓lbs salmon (in one long strip if possible)
1 tsp fennel seeds
60ml/4 tbsps grated cheese
225ml/8fl oz fish stock
30g/1oz butter
Salt and pepper

1. Make the dough by mixing together the flour, a good pinch of salt and the 3 eggs. Set the dough aside to rest for 30 minutes and then roll out very thinly into long strips.

2. Part-cook the pasta in salted, boiling water for 1 minute. Drain and then lay out on damp tea towel, without overlapping the strips.

3. Cut the salmon into thin slices – a very sharp knife with a finely serrated blade is best for this delicate job. Remove all the bones.

4. Butter an ovenproof dish and place strips of pasta into the base.

5. Now build up layers of white sauce, a few fennel seeds, the salmon, salt, pepper and then another layer of pasta. Continue layering these ingredients until they are all used, finishing with a layer of pasta.

6. Pour over the fish stock and then sprinkle over the cheese. Cook in a hot 200°C/400°F/Gas Mark 6 oven until the fish stock has been almost completely absorbed. Serve hot.

TIME: Preparation takes about 40 minutes and cooking takes approximately 35 minutes.

SERVING IDEA: This lasagne can be served with a cream sauce made by gently heating a little cream with 1 tsp fennel seeds.

COOK'S TIP: This lasagne should be slightly crisp and golden on top. If necessary, place the dish under a hot grill for 1 minute.

TORTELLINI

*Vary the amount of Parmesan cheese in
this recipe to suit your own taste.*

SERVES 4

Dough
300g/10oz strong plain flour
Pinch of salt
1 tbsp water
1 tbsp oil
3 eggs

Filling
2 tbsps cream cheese
1 cooked chicken breast, finely diced
2 tbsps ham, finely diced
2 spinach leaves, stalks discarded, cooked
    and chopped finely
1 tbsp grated Parmesan cheese
1 egg, beaten
Salt
Pepper

Sauce
280ml/½ pint cream
60g/2oz mushrooms, cleaned and sliced
60g/2oz Parmesan cheese, grated
1 tbsp chopped parsley
Salt
Pepper

Filling

1. Beat the cream cheese until soft and smooth. Add chicken, ham, spinach and Parmesan cheese, and mix well. Add egg gradually, and salt and pepper to taste. Set aside.

Dough

1. Sift flour and salt onto a board. Make a well in the centre. Mix water, oil and lightly beaten eggs together, and gradually pour into well, working in the flour with the other hand, a little at a time. Continue until the mixture comes together in a firm ball of dough.

2. Knead on a lightly-floured board for 5 minutes, or until smooth and elastic. Put into a bowl, cover with a cloth, and leave to stand for 15 minutes.

3. Roll dough out on a lightly-floured board as thinly as possible. Using a 2 inch cutter, cut out circles. Put ½ teaspoon of filling into the centre of each circle. Fold in half, pressing edges together firmly. Wrap around forefinger, and press ends together. Cook in batches in a large pan, in plenty of boiling salted water for about 10 minutes until tender, stirring occasionally.

Sauce

1. Meanwhile, gently heat cream in a pan. Add mushrooms, Parmesan cheese, parsley, and salt and pepper to taste. Gently cook for 3 minutes.

To serve, toss sauce together with tortellini and sprinkle with parsley.

TIME: Preparation takes 30 minutes and cooking takes 15 minutes.

MEAT RAVIOLI

*Preparing your own pasta dough is very satisfying as it
almost always tastes better than the shop-bought variety.*

SERVES 4

Dough
275g/9oz strong plain flour
Pinch of salt
3 eggs

Filling
60g/2oz butter or margarine
1 clove garlic, crushed
1 onion, peeled and grated
225g/8oz minced beef
75ml/5 tbsps red wine
Salt
Pepper
2 tbsps breadcrumbs
120g/4oz cooked spinach, chopped
2 eggs, beaten

Sauce
400g/14 oz tin plum tomatoes
1 small onion, peeled and grated
1 small carrot, diced finely
1 bay leaf
3 parsley stalks
Salt
Pepper

60g/2oz Parmesan cheese, grated

Filling

1. Heat butter in pan. Add garlic and onion, and fry gently for 1 minute. Add minced beef, and fry until browned. Add red wine, and salt and pepper to taste, and cook uncovered for 15 minutes.

2. Strain juices and reserve them for sauce. Allow to cool.

3. Add breadcrumbs, chopped spinach, and beaten eggs to bind.

4. Adjust salt and pepper to taste.

Dough

1. Sift flour in a bowl with salt. Make a well in the centre and add the eggs. Work flour and eggs together with a spoon, then knead by hand, until a smooth dough is formed. Leave dough to rest for 15 minutes.

2. Lightly flour board, and roll out dough thinly into a rectangle. Cut dough in half.

3. Shape the filling into small balls, and set them about 1½ inches apart on one half of the dough.

4. Place the other half on top, and cut with a ravioli cutter or small pastry cutter. Seal the edges.

5. Cook in batches in a large, wide pan with plenty of boiling salted water until tender – about 8 minutes. Remove carefully with a perforated spoon. Meanwhile, make the sauce.

Sauce

1. Put all the sauce ingredients in a saucepan. Add juice from cooked meat, and bring to boil. Simmer for 10 minutes. Push through a sieve, and return smooth sauce to pan. Adjust seasoning.

To serve, put ravioli in a warm dish and cover with tomato sauce. Serve immediately, with grated Parmesan cheese.

TIME: Preparation takes 30 minutes and cooking takes 5 minutes.

FETTUCINE ESCARGOTS WITH LEEKS AND SUN-DRIED TOMATOES

These dried tomatoes keep for a long time, and allow you to add a sunny taste to dishes whatever the time of year.

SERVES 4-6

6 sun-dried tomatoes or 6 fresh Italian
  plum tomatoes
400g/14oz tinned escargots (snails), drained
340g/12oz fresh or dried whole-wheat
  fettucine (tagliatelle)
3 tbsps olive oil
2 cloves garlic, crushed
1 large or 2 small leeks, trimmed, split,
  well washed and finely sliced
6 oyster, shittake or other large mushrooms
60ml/4 tbsps chicken or vegetable stock
3 tbsps dry white wine
90ml/6 tbsps double cream
2 tsps chopped fresh basil
2 tsps chopped fresh parsley
Salt and pepper

1. To 'sun-dry' tomatoes in the oven, cut the tomatoes in half lengthwise.

2. Use a teaspoon or your finger to scoop out about half the seeds and juice. Press gently with your palm to flatten slightly. Sprinkle both sides with salt and place tomatoes, cut side up, on a rack over a baking pan.

3. Place in the oven on the lowest possible setting, with door ajar, if necessary, for 24 hours, checking after 12 hours. Allow to dry until no liquid is left and the tomatoes are firm. Chop roughly.

4. Drain the escargots well and dry with paper towels.

5. Place the fettucine in boiling salted water and cook for about 10-12 minutes, or until al dente. Drain, rinse under hot water and leave in a colander to drain dry.

6. Meanwhile, heat the olive oil in a frying pan and add the garlic and leeks. Cook slowly to soften slightly. Add the mushrooms and cook until the leeks are tender crisp. Remove to a plate. Add the drained escargots to the pan and cook over high heat for about 2 minutes, stirring constantly.

7. Pour on the stock and wine and bring to the boil. Boil to reduce by about a quarter and add the cream and tomatoes. Bring to the boil then cook slowly for about 3 minutes. Add the herbs, salt and pepper to taste.

8. Add the leeks, mushrooms and fettucine to the pan and heat through. Serve immediately.

TIME: Preparation takes about 24 hours for the tomatoes to dry and about 15-20 minutes to finish the dish.

LASAGNE NAPOLETANA

This is a lasagne as it is cooked and eaten in Naples.
With its layer of red, green and white it looks as delicious
as it tastes and is very easy to prepare.

SERVES 6

9 sheets spinach lasagne pasta

Tomato Sauce
3 tbsps olive oil
2 cloves garlic, crushed
900g/2lbs fresh tomatoes, peeled, or
    tinned tomatoes, drained
2 tbsps chopped fresh basil, six whole
    leaves reserved
Salt and pepper
Pinch sugar

Cheese filling
450g/1lb ricotta cheese
60g/4 tbsps unsalted butter
225g/8oz Mozzarella cheese, grated
Salt and pepper
Pinch nutmeg

1. Cook the pasta for 8 minutes in boiling salted water with 1 tbsp oil. Drain and rinse under hot water and place in a single layer on a damp cloth. Cover with another damp cloth and set aside.

2. To prepare the sauce, cook the garlic in remaining oil for about 1 minute in a large saucepan. When pale brown, add the tomatoes, basil, salt, pepper and sugar. If using fresh tomatoes, drop into boiling water for 6-8 seconds. Transfer to cold water and leave to cool completely. This will make the peels easier to remove.

3. Lower the heat under the saucepan and simmer the sauce for 35 minutes. Add more seasoning or sugar to taste.

4. Beat the ricotta cheese and butter together until creamy and stir into the remaining sauce ingredients.

5. To assemble the lasagne, oil a rectangular baking dish and place 3 sheets of lasagne on the base. Cover with one third of the sauce and carefully spread on a layer of cheese. Place another 3 layers of pasta over the cheese and cover with another third of the sauce. Add the remaining cheese filling and cover with the remaining pasta. Spoon the remaining sauce on top.

6. Cover with foil and bake for 20 minutes at 190°C/375°F/Gas Mark 5. Uncover and cook for 10 minutes longer. Garnish with the reserved leaves and leave to stand for 10-15 minutes before serving.

TIME: Preparation takes about 25 minutes and cooking takes about 1-1¼ hours.

LAMB WITH PASTA AND TOMATOES

*Lamb appears in many different guises – here it has an Italian
influence with pasta, herbs and Parmesan cheese in this recipe.*

SERVES 6-8

1 leg or shoulder of lamb
2 cloves garlic, peeled and cut into thin
   slivers
60ml/4 tbsps olive oil
450g/1lb fresh tomatoes or 400g/14oz
   tinned tomatoes
1 tbsp chopped fresh oregano
Salt and pepper
570ml/1 pint lamb or beef stock or water
225g/8oz pasta shells or spirals
Finely grated Parmesan cheese

1. Cut slits about 5cm/2 inch intervals all over the lamb. Insert small slivers of garlic into each slit. Place the lamb in a large baking dish and rub the surface with the olive oil.

2. Cook in a preheated oven at 220°C/425°F/Gas Mark 7 for about 50 minutes, basting occasionally.

3. Meanwhile, parboil the pasta for about 5 minutes and rinse in hot water to remove the starch.

4. Turn the meat over and add the stock or water, pasta and additional seasoning. Mix the tomatoes with the oregano, salt and pepper and pour over the lamb. Stir well. Cook an additional 20-30 minutes, stirring the pasta occasionally to ensure even cooking.

5. When the pasta is completely cooked, turn the lamb over again and sprinkle with cheese to serve. Serve directly from the dish or transfer to a large, deep serving plate.

TIME: Preparation takes about 20 minutes and cooking takes about 1 hour 35 minutes.

VARIATION: The dish can be made without tomatoes, if desired. Beef can be substituted for the lamb and the cooking time increased.

ITALIAN CASSEROLE

Serve this hearty main course with a
green salad or broccoli and fresh bread.

SERVES 4

90g/3oz small macaroni
60g/2oz butter or margarine
1 clove garlic, crushed
1 onion, peeled and chopped
2 x 400g/14oz tins plum tomatoes
1 tbsp tomato purée
1 red pepper, cored, seeds removed, and
   chopped roughly
1 green pepper, cored, seeds removed,
   and chopped roughly
225g/8oz salami, cut into chunks
10 black olives, halved, and stones
   removed
120g/4oz Mozzarella cheese, sliced thinly
Salt
Pepper

1. Cook the macaroni in plenty of boiling salted water for 10 minutes, or until tender but still firm. Rinse under hot water and drain well. Place in a shallow, oven-proof dish.

2. Meanwhile, heat butter in pan, and fry onion and garlic gently until soft.

3. Add undrained tomatoes, tomato purée, red and green peppers, salami and olives, and stir well. Simmer uncovered for 5 minutes. Season with salt and pepper.

4. Pour over the macaroni, stir, and cover with the sliced cheese. Bake uncovered in a moderate oven for 20 minutes, until cheese has melted. Serve immediately.

TIME: Preparation takes 15 minutes and cooking takes 40 minutes.

SPINACH LASAGNE

Everyone will be asking for seconds when
they discover the taste of this delicious lasagne.

SERVES 4

8 sheets green lasagne pasta

Spinach sauce
90g/3oz butter or margarine
90g/3oz flour
140ml/¼ pint milk
325g/11oz packet of frozen spinach,
   thawed and chopped finely
Pinch of ground nutmeg
Salt
Pepper

Mornay sauce
30g/1oz butter or margarine
30g/1oz flour
280ml/½ pint milk
90g/3oz Parmesan cheese, grated
1 tsp French mustard
Salt

Spinach sauce

1. Heat butter in pan, stir in flour and cook gently for 30 seconds.

2. Remove from heat, and stir in milk gradually. Return to heat, and bring to the boil, stirring continuously. Cook for 3 minutes.

3. Add spinach, nutmeg, and salt and pepper to taste. Set aside.

Cook spinach lasagne in lots of boiling salted water for 10 minutes, or until tender. Rinse in cold water, and drain carefully. Dry on a clean cloth.

Mornay sauce

1. Heat butter in pan and stir in flour, cooking for 30 seconds.

2. Remove from heat, and stir in milk. Return to heat, stirring continuously, until boiling. Continue stirring, and simmer for 3 minutes.

3. Draw off heat, add mustard, two-thirds of cheese, and salt to taste.

Preheat oven to 200°C/400°F/Gas Mark 7. Grease an oven-proof baking dish. Line the base with a layer of lasagne, followed by some of the spinach mixture, and a layer of the cheese sauce. Repeat the process, finishing with a layer of lasagne and with a covering of cheese sauce. Sprinkle with the remaining cheese. Bake in a hot oven until golden on top. Serve immediately.

TIME: Preparation takes 10 minutes and cooking takes 30 minutes.

VANILLA CREAM MELBA

Soup pasta is enhanced with a delicious raspberry sauce and peaches in this easy-to-prepare dessert.

SERVES 4

90g/3oz soup pasta
450ml/¾ pint milk
45g/1½ oz brown sugar
Few drops vanilla essence
140ml/¼ pint cream, lightly whipped
1 tin peach halves
1 tsp cinnamon

Melba sauce
225g/8oz raspberries
30g/1oz icing sugar

1. Cook pasta in milk and sugar until soft. Stir regularly, being careful not to allow it to boil over. Remove from heat and stir in vanilla essence.

2. Pour pasta into a bowl to cool. When cool, fold in cream. Chill.

3. Meanwhile, make melba sauce. Push raspberries through a sieve. Mix in icing sugar to desired thickness and taste.

4. Serve pasta with peach halves and melba sauce. Dust with cinnamon if desired.

TIME: Preparation takes 15 minutes and cooking takes 10 minutes.

BLACK CHERRY RAVIOLI WITH SOURED CREAM SAUCE

*A simple dough is mixed with cherries and
cream to make the perfect ending to a meal.*

SERVES 4

Dough

275g/9oz strong plain flour
1 tbsp sugar
3 eggs, lightly beaten

Large can black cherries, pips removed
60g/2oz granulated sugar
1 tsp arrowroot
120ml/4fl oz soured cream
120ml/4fl oz double cream

1. Put cherries in a sieve. Strain off juice and reserve.

2. Make dough by sifting flour and sugar in a bowl. Make a well in the centre and add lightly-beaten eggs. Work flour and eggs together with a spoon, and then by hand, until a smooth dough is formed. Knead gently.

3. Lightly flour board, and roll dough out thinly into a rectangle. Cut dough in half. Put well-drained cherries about 4cm (1½ inches) apart on the dough.

4. Place the other half on top, and cut with a small glass or pastry cutter. Seal well around edges with back of a fork.

5. Boil plenty of water in a large saucepan, and drop in cherry pasta. Cook for about 10 minutes, or until they rise to the surface. Remove with a draining spoon and keep warm. Keep 2 tablespoons cherry juice aside.

6. Mix 1 tablespoon cherry juice with arrowroot; mix remaining juice with sugar and set over heat. Add arrowroot mixture, and heat until it thickens.

7. Meanwhile mix soured cream and double cream together, and marble 1 tablespoon of cherry juice through it.

8. Pour hot, thickened cherry juice over cherry ravioli. Serve hot with cream sauce.

TIME: Preparation takes 30 minutes and cooking takes 15 minutes.

CHOCOLATE CREAM HELÈNE

*Pears, cream and pasta combine perfectly
in this simply delicious dessert.*

SERVES 4

90g/3oz soup pasta
450ml/¾ pint milk
45g/1½ oz caster sugar
1 tsp cocoa
140ml/¼ pint cream, lightly whipped
1 tbsp hot water
1 large tin pear halves

Garnish
Chocolate, grated

1. Cook pasta in milk and sugar until soft.
Stir regularly, being careful not to allow it
to boil over.

2. Meanwhile, dissolve cocoa in hot water,
and stir into pasta.

3. Pour pasta into a bowl to cool, when
cool, fold in lightly-whipped cream. Chill.
Serve with pear halves, and a sprinkling of
grated chocolate.

TIME: Preparation takes 15 minutes and cooking takes 10 minutes.

Index